Fascination Series
A Curriculum and Planning Journal

WOOD

Fascination of Earth
Nature-Based Inquiries for Children

By Dr. Claire Warden

Many thanks to the members of the Auchlone Kindergarten team, both past and present, for their contribution and in making this book possible.

Special thanks goes to all the children for whom we are in contact with on a daily basis for their joy and inspiration.

For further information about Mindstretchers publications and the full range of learning resources, email inquiries@mindstretchers.academy.

www.mindstretchers.academy

FOREWORD
by Leif Christensen

Senior Lecturer – Outdoor Pedagogy
University College Lillebaelt, Denmark

This little book is a rich mine of educational reflections and practical hints concerning safety, materials, and tools. It is the latest example of the pioneering work done by Dr. Claire Warden and the Mindstretchers Academy to promote outdoor pedagogy in all its forms.

This book discusses the material of wood and then explores the handling of that wood in great detail through children's fascination of changing its shape with tools (whittling) and remodeling through cutting it up or attaching other things to it. Probably one of the best-known "whittlers" in Scandinavia is Emil of Lönneberga, the main character in a series of children's novels by Astrid Lindgren (the Swedish author who also wrote the *Pippi Longstocking* books). Emil has a prodigious knack for getting into trouble. When his boyish pranks misfire, he runs away and locks himself in the toolshed or, if he doesn't make it on time, is locked in there by his father as a punishment. However, Emil does not regard this as a punishment as he spends the time in the shed carving figures out of pieces of wood - 369 figures in all over the course of time. Emil's activities in the toolshed contribute considerably to his general education, and he is described as a very intelligent, creative, and resourceful person.

Such qualities were also possessed by the Viking craftsmen. The work they did was characterized by the Scandinavian word "Sløjd" ("Nordic Sloyd"), which is more or less synonymous with the terms "craft" in English, though with the added idea that a person who was good at "Sløjd" was also "crafty" and artful.

These two examples show a strong connection between manual activities and the character traits of those who practice them. There is a Danish saying that can be quoted in this context: "The products of the hand are the footprints of the soul."

So, whittling is a very serious matter indeed!

Many people are, of course, aware that whittling is a very relaxing, multi-sensory activity, but there is much more to the story than this.

Norwegian educational researcher Arne Trageton has shown that children's constructive play of, for example, working with actual materials such as clay, sand, and wood stimulates their social, linguistic, and cognitive development. Since I consider the process of whittling, in which various materials are worked on using a tool, to be a more developed form of constructive play, I would expect children's social, linguistic, and cognitive skills to be even more stimulated by this process.

I am gratified to see that this book situates the activity of whittling within a broader context. When the hands-on experience gained through working with the hands is placed in a cultural-historical perspective and linked to related areas such as sustainability, the result is improved learning and increased motivation.

Contents

Introduction
To The Fascination Series

Welcome to this series of nature-based curriculum and planning journals which have a beautiful combination of theory, curriculum, and reflection. You will be able to confidently embrace a more planet-centered way of educating children through collecting and completing this unique series of books. They will:

- Improve planning by providing pages of hundreds of possibilities to talk about with children;

- Improve engagement through inquiry-based learning in the Floorbooks®; and

- Improve the quality of time you and children spend indoors and outdoors, so they become the stewards of the planet in the future.

When I work with colleagues worldwide who want to develop their nature-based practice, the message I hear is that there are challenges around planning and curriculum that have made it a dull and uninspiring process. So my goal is to bring the joy back to engaging with curriculum and planning through these journals so that we use Floorbooks® as a child-centered planning approach.

We need an approach to planning so that both adults and children spend time together rather than being overloaded with paperwork. Floorbooks® are a way of planning with and for children that also ensures we are accountable to a framework in a curriculum to ensure we are covering skills, knowledge, and concepts in a way that helps children develop a positive attitude to learning. These journals will give the guidance and support needed to move forward with enthusiasm and, therefore, improve the experience for yourself and the children you work with.

Some questions we explore in this series include:

- What is nature pedagogy all about?

- How do we plan in a child-centered way?

- Is there a way for pedagogy and paperwork to align?

- How do I cover academics when I go outside?

- What do children learn when they play with materials?

- How do I keep children safe enough?

- How can I build my confidence in planning for nature-based experiences?

- How can I share the learning with children and families?

The journals are part of a much broader set of opportunities and training on the www.Mindstretchers.academy where you can collect training certificates in both nature pedagogy and inquiry-based work through the internationally acclaimed Floorbook® approach.

Introduction to Wood

Walking between and under trees has to be one of the most delightful experiences. Humans have benefitted from trees in so many ways from shelter to a sustainable material, and yet we are only now beginning to become more aware of their greater role in our lives. They are storage vessels of carbon, they mitigate the impact of the sun's rays on our skin, and they are quite literally the lungs of the planet. Encounters with trees and plants start from a young age as the dappled light they create stimulates the infant mind to the discovery of seeds by a two-year old who begins to become aware of the human and other-than-human worlds.

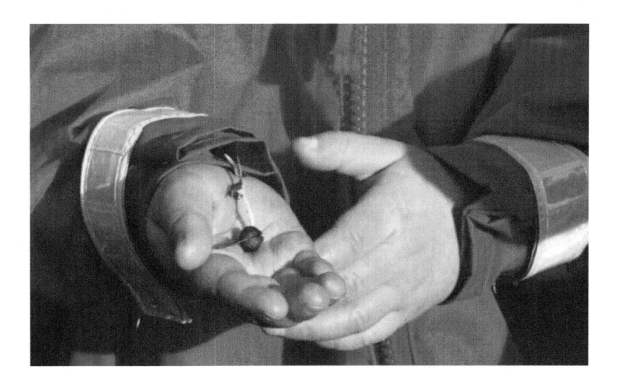

A tree has a high play affordance as defined by Nicholson in 1971. It offers or affords so many possibilities that it has a very high value in children's play. It is both a place to play in and on but also play under in the shadows. A tree has a sense of gravitas, and the size and scale of them help us all to have a sense of place.

Trees provide a wealth of loose materials such as leaves, sticks, seeds, stems, and bark that can be gathered sustainably and accessed for most of the year and they create a habitat for a wide variety of insects and animals. We all need to increase the number of trees in our lives.

Our creative relationship with trees has been represented in many ways from the use of wood to make paper that we then used through time to record our ideas and stories in to the homes we designed and built to resources we have manufactured or hand carved. Trees are represented by children across cultures and climates with a variety of media. The question is do we understand the value of trees and spend enough time really celebrating the possibilities of encounters specifically with wood.

Children find fascinating moments, materials, and objects every day, but sometimes the pressure of a rigid curriculum means that we don't follow them. Instead, we follow a pathway created by an adult who doesn't know you, your children, or your place. There is a middle pathway that allows childrens ideas to fill the pages of our planning but also gives us support to know how far to go, how to manage many different fascinations, and when to step intentionally to extend thinking. The *point of flow* is a state of mind which is all encompassing and is linked to higher order thinking. It was developed in the work of Csíkszentmihályi (1990) and two of the aspects that help them to reach that focussed engaged state is that it is purposeful and complex. Exploring and playing with wood is both purposeful and complex.

In many parts of the world, using and handling wood has been used across education in a variety of ways. Given the opportunity, we see children learning to stack wooden blocks, making shelters and dens, collecting special bits of driftwood on a beach, creating something at a woodwork bench, or sitting quietly with a tool hand carving a stick. Wood is one of the first materials we gathered as humans due to its flexibility, and, if harvested sustainably, will be part of our solution into the future.

This book will provide the foundational knowledge about wood. For many of us, our link to it as a material is often through objects in our home, and yet it can be a context for play and discover; it truly is a material that will help us to create sustainable environments.

Children need time to "be", to process and to consider the world around them, and to allow an enquiring mind to follow its own fascinations so that it can reach a deeper connection. That means that we slow down the content of a curriculum and allow the skills and capacities of life long learning to be learned. Our role in this process is to be alongside children stepping in and out as they need us or when we feel that greater intent may deepen or support children's thinking.

Sometimes it is hard to define what we do as it is complex and situated. These journals are designed to be a collaboration of my guide and the ideas children have shared and reflections on your own experience.

Claire

Dr. Claire Warden

1
What is Woodworking?

Within the context of this book, woodworking is the broad term used to describe how children engage with wood as an open-ended material that can be worked or used to create other objects. The use of sticks and leaves offers so much potential in their own right that they are the subject of further planning books, but, as we know, all that the nature of play affordance is that they cannot be truly separated within children's play and discovery.

This text explores the larger pieces of wood, both discovered and manufactured, and the way that we can use them effectively as part of a child-led inquiry. The introduction of tools comes quite naturally when children move into the sphere of design and construction as they offer a greater complexity and process. The introduction of sandpaper alone can absorb children in smoothing a found stick or rounding the edges of a lump of wood, and when the process of abrasion is extended into rasps and files, the engagement continues and the mastery of the skill develops.

There is much debate about whether whittling is in fact wood carving or whether they are two separate things. In general, we might think of wood carvers who use more complex tools such as gouges or chisels whereas a whittler may simply use a pocket knife and a small piece of wood to make a creative shape of some kind. Outlining this distinction is perhaps unnecessary at this point as they both involve the art of working with wood. It is an area that is both large and varied and very much worth exploring with all groups over a long period of time.

Many of us have heard or even used the term to "whittle away the hours", but perhaps we have not thought about where this term has derived from. When we say to 'whittle away the hours", we make reference to the traditional art of whittling in which a person uses a sharp implement to shave off pieces from a chunk of wood and create a new shape out of it. The time passes as the whittler becomes fully involved in the process. Whittling has always been a fascination for children; I am sure we can all remember at least one child who was ever so keen to get their first Swiss army knife and then carried it around with them everywhere as they played in the garden and explored the outside world.

What can you whittle?

Popular items for people to make when whittling generally include cooking implements such as spoons, forks, and knives, crockery such as plates and bowls, or representations of animals like birds and fish. One artist, Chris Lubekmann, specializes in whittling the ends of sticks and twigs to create figures, pen tops, and animals which can be found in his book *The Art of Whittling*. Making spoons and bowls, for example, requires carving out the wood into a convex shape which can appear difficult to begin with but, once experience has been gained in using the curved edges of the knife, this can be achieved with a bit of perseverance. More basic projects that can be achieved with simple whittling skills, such as those with a Lancashire potato peeler, mainly involve whittling away bark to make breadsticks, picture frames, or sharpening the end of a stick to make a marshmallow stick, mud pencil or a spear.

Art and Industry

Whittling, or wood carving, has been around since ancient times. Cavemen, for example, would have shaped wood using sharp stones to make tools and weapons, and examples of people working with wood for both decorative and functional aims span across history. For example, evidence of the finely detailed Egyptian wood carving techniques that were used to create hieroglyphics and figures can be seen today in museums. In Scotland, we have a tradition of standing stones; many Celtic crosses still exist in villages such as Fowlis Wester near Crieff in Perthshire. The use of carving and whittling techniques to create artworks to honor religious icons or to decorate places of worship, such as churches and mosques, is vast, and one can find many examples when visiting such places. Such examples can be found in the work of the famous Swiss artist Tilman Riemenschneider.

From the seventeenth century, wood was used more and more domestically for creating tables, staircases, room paneling, and bed posts. The introduction of wood carving machinery essentially put an end to the individual craftsmanship of the artist in this area and opened up the beginning of the timber industry that we see today.

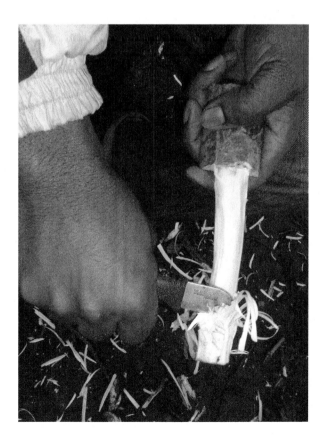

Using Wood as a Sustainable Resource

Wood carving and whittling is seen by many today as a pastime and indeed in modern times, and it is associated very much with the "folk scene" of getting back to free and traditional ways of living and working and connecting with the natural environment. It is used by most groups who engage in Forest Schools in this country as a core part of the creative skills that can be developed in natural spaces. Beach School areas that have access to driftwood have created shelters and dens that use the elements to create characters to embellish their spaces.

Woodworking

Shaping and making objects from wood has been a human pastime. There is often a point where children want to change the shape of the wood. The use of tools develops a wide range of possibilities from functional spoons to games to decorations as can be seen in the case studies.

Tools

In terms of whittling implements, it is recommended in all literature associated with whittling that you use a sharp knife, with an emphasis on the fact that it must be sharp! If you have ever tried carving anything from wood to a loaf of bread with a blunt knife, you will know how important this is. It is often assumed that sharper knives are the ones that put us most at risk and are the most likely to cause injuries. However, when we explore this issue, we will realize that this is a misconception and that sharp knives are actually safer. This is usually because if you have a sharp knife, it will actually cut into what you are trying to carve rather than slipping onto a softer surface like your skin. People will recommend many different types of knives for carving with. For example, Scandinavian scouting uses fixed blade knives, fold up pen knives, or even Stanley knives. We generally use fixed blade knives that have a small sharp blade at the end.

In terms of working with children in schools, however, we generally use Lancashire potato peelers. Although they seemingly lack the impact of a pen knife, these implements work exceptionally well for introducing whittling to a group of younger children. The short, fixed blade is used as the skill level increases, and the peelers have done their job in teaching some of the procedures that wrap around safe handling. Tools themselves are many and varied. The visual mind map here provides an overview of some of the tools used. The underlying aspect is that the tool is a way of achieving a design or a creative plan that children have thought through themselves. There are certainly intentional teaching moments where and how to use the tool is explained, but it needs to be in the context of nature based pedagogy which is child-centered.

Creating a Space for Wood

All models of education are driven by interactions, environments, and experiences. To understand how we can create really effective and high quality provision, we can use the idea of the four points of a star to help us consider what we need to consider. These are picked up again in the journal pages for you to make notes.

Space - Where will the space or area be? How will you link the locations of inside, outside, and beyond the gate of your setting? How will you support gender neutrality in your images and decor?

Time - How long will you give children to work on a project? Where will you store the work-in-progress? How will you help children remember their ideas? Will there be a planning wall? A Floorbook®?

Adult Role - What language will you use in the interactions to widen and deepen children's knowledge and understanding? How confident is the team about the language of wood?

Resources - Where will you source the wood? Is it sustainable? Are driftwood and natural shapes openly accessible for small world landscapes? Will you start with a soft wood like Balsa or use Pine straight away? Will you provide a range of screws and nails or use broad headed tacks first? How will you aid the tidy up process - an outline board, counting systems, picture charts to match to?

Types of Wood

Working with wood starts with understanding what properties the wood offers us. Children gather this knowledge through encountering wood in many different locations, such as floating on water, rotting in a bug habitat, or in a living form as branches and trees. When we then come to choose it or make choices about using it, they make informed choices. When it comes to choosing a wood, try to use softwoods such as pine as they are easier to work with. Hardwoods, such as Beech and Oak, can be more challenging to use with whittling and shaping.

To work with wood, you need to understand the nature of the materials you are using. The grain of the wood is a result of the way that the wood grows at different speeds during the year, creating layers known as growth rings. In terms of whittling skills, we talk about the direction of the grain. In very basic terms, it can be summed up as follows:

- Against the grain – this can be hard work and cause the wood to tear; and

- With the grain – this is easier and allows for a cleaner finish.

Ways to Whittle

There is something very engaging about uncovering new surfaces, and many younger children enjoy using their fingers in peeling the bark off green branches like Willow or Hazel. The bright new wood and the flexible strips of bark then become a play material in their own way.

Driftwood is a gift as it has already been cleaned and shaped by the sea. Collected responsibly, they are nature's treasures with their own basket and place on the shelf. Handling these pieces of wood is full of discovery, from the holes where a knot used to be to the smooth edges and the salty smell that comes from them.

When children are ready to use a tool, there are a number of different techniques that can be used.

When whittling, the first technique is the forward stroke, which is what we generally use with our children and the technique which best suits the use of a Lancashire peeler, where the blade runs in the same line as a knife. In using this method, the children are taught to always work the tool away from themselves, and this works effectively for whittling off bark and sharpening the end of sticks.

A girl aged three using the straight forward away stroke.

Another technique is the draw stroke, whereby the whittler grips the piece of wood firmly, bracing the tool hand with the thumb against the wood. Very precisely, the whittler then cuts towards the body, keeping short and controlled strokes throughout.

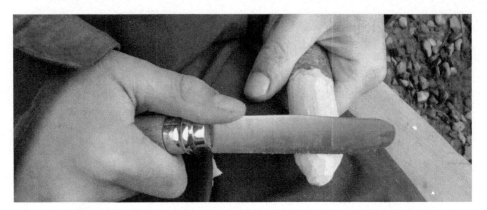

Using a rasp to smooth edges and contour the wood.

An adult participant using a push stroke.

Another common stroke is the push stroke, where the whittler uses the thumb from the other hand to gently push the blade on the knife forward away from the body. This is, again, good for controlled cuts and allows whittlers to make detailed cuts on the wood.

Journal Prompt

These pages are designed to help you build the knowledge in yourself and your team.

Space -

Where will the wood space or area be?

How will you link the locations of inside, outside and beyond the gate of your setting?

How will you support gender neutrality in your images and decor?

Journal Prompt

Time -

How long can you give children to work on a project?

Where will you store the work in progress?

How will you help children remember their ideas?

Will there be a planning wall? A Floorbook®?

Journal Prompt

Adult Role -

What language will you use in the interactions to widen and deepen children's knowledge and understanding?

How confident is the team about the use of wood in the program?

Journal Prompt

Resources -

Where will you source wood? Is it sustainable?

Are driftwood and natural shapes openly accessible for small world landscapes?

Will you start with a soft wood like Balsa or use Pine straight away?

Will you provide a range of screws and nails or use broad headed tacks first?

How will you aid the tidy up process- an outline board, counting systems, picture charts to match to?

2
Planning Possibilities

The way of working within the nature pedagogy approach is built on a foundation of co-constructivist thinking, which brings together the intentional adult and the child into a pedagogical dance (*Learning With Nature*, Warden 2015). This means that there are times when the adult leads play and learning and others when the child leads. This is the balance we try to achieve to ensure that the adult has the awareness of the curriculum and milestones that are developmentally appropriate while consulting and empowering children through recording and acting upon their ideas, plans and theories.

The activity of planning should be a joyful thing as it is full of the possibilities of the things to come. When we think about what we can do for children, we are, in essence, planning. When we record this dynamic process in a format that can easily be accessed by other members of the team, it starts to guide group experiences and opportunities. There are a number of things to reflect upon as we explore this playful, inquiry-based approach, such as:

- How do you decide what to do in your program?

- To what extent do you use children's ideas in the program rather than all your own?

- Is there a clear link between what children say, do, make or write and the actions you take in your planning?

- Some children are not always aware of the choices and possibilities they have in the setting. How do you support all children to be aware of the things they could do? How do you start the conversation?

Using Floorbooks® is part of the solution as they are focussed on planning with and for children (*Planning With and For Children*, Warden 2020). There are four strategies that are key to planning in this way:

- The Floorbook®- a large book that is the central hub for working documentation;

- The Talking Tub- a box of provocations created that is linked to Lines of Inquiry;

- The Family Books- individual evidence of the learning that are available to children; and

- The Daily Diary- operational planning and observation notes collated by staff linked to the Floorbook®/ Family Books.

The difference between a Floorbook® and a large scrapbook is that it is guided by wide Lines of Inquiry, or main ideas, that are being explored by children. It has defined features that increase its value to being central to the planning process. When children's play experiences flow and link together, it makes more sense and, therefore, makes it easier to learn. Some of the possibilities are shared in this chapter as visual mind maps for both tool use and projects with wood.

Line of Inquiry

The myriad of conversations that take place in a group of children all have value and purpose, but sometimes as the educator we can identify an underlying Line of Inquiry. This is a fascination that persists over time and becomes a central idea that is explored in many ways through the duration of the inquiry.

The Line of Inquiry or central idea has some characteristics that support us to understand if we have reached it:

- The central idea is written in one sentence (e.g. the change in direction of a line);

- It expresses concisely an enduring understanding (e.g. the inquiry explored a link between a material and movement);

- It is substantial enough to generate in–depth inquiries (e.g. materials and movement is broad enough for depth but not as wide as the whole of movement);

- An effective Line of Inquiry is often concept driven such as change;

- It is relevant, engaging, and significant; and

- It allows for action to be taken in a way that makes sense to children.

 The Talking Tub

Having tangible objects for children to touch and explore has a direct link to their engagement and vocabulary. Through offering a nature-centered Talking Tub, we can explore curriculum subjects through a context that is exciting and motivational. When the children talk about the objects, the adults record their ideas in the

Floorbook® as quotes or through film and audio as a QR code to bring together digital and hard copy documentation.

The materials stay in the Talking Tub and are for use at a gathering time with adults. This means that more fragile elements can be included.

The table below gives the Lines of Inquiry and suggests materials and objects to collect to deepen the conversations you have with children. The contents change according to the age of the children, their interests and how the inquiry moves along.

Wood as a material is used widely across the world. This inquiry started out with a Talking Tub on wood as a material and took us on a journey to explore the skill of whittling and then to make a range of artifacts.

The adaptation of the Talking Tub to follow the children's interests deepens the conversation and ensures that the curriculum is loose enough that children can play and explore the things that fascinate them.

Fascination of Earth: Wood

Line of Inquiry	Objects	Wondering/Inquiry Questions
Knowledge of types of wood	• Chart outlining differing softwoods and hardwoods • Examples of hardwoods and softwoods • A selection of sticks (dried and green) and bark	Where does it come from?
Structure of wood	• Cross-section diagrams of the growth rings	What is wood? What are the rings in the tree? How do they get there?
Creation of artifacts Decoration/homes/ games/moving objects (see visual mind map)	• Stick, string, wire, feathers, and leaves to create artifacts • Images of some things to make from previous groups of children or from wider selection such as bowls, chairs, stars, models etc.	How could we use wood to make something? How could you make a ….? What could we use?
ID of trees in the area	• Examples of bark if fallen to the ground • ID charts • Images taken by children of *their* trees (ones they have near them at home or in their setting)	What names do we have for trees? (Expect personal names and sci-entific ones)
Use of tools when we work with wood inside and outside (see visual mind map)	• Examples of tools that could be used-draw saw, glove, peelers to take off green bark, nails, screws etc. • Image of the store area/ tool wrap for tools to discuss safe handling and care	How do you use these things? Let's look for clues as to what they might be for. How can we look after them?
Awareness of the role of trees	• Images of trees in a variety of states of health. • Seasonal images are relevant to the climate where you live. • Wood for stove/ wooden artifacts from the home (e.g. spoon)	Why do we share the earth with trees? Where could we find a tree? Where could we find something made of wood?
Language of trees	• Stimulus for language related to the natural world • Images of trees with a focus on appearance • Expand to pull in vocabulary linked to the experiences that children have had	Use a range of rich vocabulary talking about wood and artifacts. I wonder why all trees look different? How would it feel to be at the top of a tree? Which is your favorite tree in the park?
Beauty of wood	• Images of art works featuring trees or wooden elements in a variety of media • Real examples of beautiful wooden artifacts to handle	What do you think about these pictures/ things? How long do you think it took to make them?

Visual Mind Maps

A visual mind map is used to offer some of the possibilities to children. It is created by the adult who should include the experiences that previous groups of children have shown an interest in.

- The visual mind map is usually created through a material encounter, such as wood.

- Children can draw and add their ideas to the visual mind map during the session.

- Children decode the map themselves using the images.

- Adults can use photos to embellish the mind map rather than hand drawings.

- A smaller version of the mind map plan is included in the Floorbook® so that more ideas can be added around it to extend existing Lines of Inquiry.

The adult can, of course, create a two dimensional mind map with children. If it is challenging to engage all the children and gather everyone's ideas, using the Talking Tub allows the adult to note interest in an object or an image through watching their engagement or choice of image or object alongside noting down what they say.

Standard question and answer sessions create a challenging space for most children to share what they know as there is no context to frame the conversation. It really is essential to create a space for talk that is full of irresistible stimuli; the visual mind map can be used as part of this provision.

The need for separation of the experiences and opportunities is really an adult concept as play and learning is holistic by its very nature. For ease this book provides two ways of looking at planning:

- Inquiry-driven

- Curriculum-led

This chapter links and connects learning in a context and it subdivides learning into curriculum subject areas in the following chapter. If you work in an environment that requires planning by a defined subject, the Lines of Inquiry could be all academic rather than broader contextual concepts as shared in the example here. How can we really note down the learning from hugging a tree as it brings everything together? We can interact to sway the conversation to have a lens on an aspect of curriculum, but often children feel emotion, consider size and dimension, understand the texture of the bark, think in language, and notice a bug all at the same moment.

There are two mind maps on the pages that follow:

1. The first explores the process of making, which connects to the idea that it is the process of shaping and altering wood that engages children. Children have so many ideas that adults need to step back and listen to their plans before they create step by step instructions for them to follow. If the adult wants to teach a skill, they can, of course, but time and space in the curriculum needs to be given to creativity and problem solving as processes that do not focus on the end product.

2. The second explores the possibilities of using tools. The introduction of tools extends the possibilities, and in many programs, the children from 3 years old have access to a basic set of tools that are then extended when the child and adult decide that they can be used appropriately and cared for.

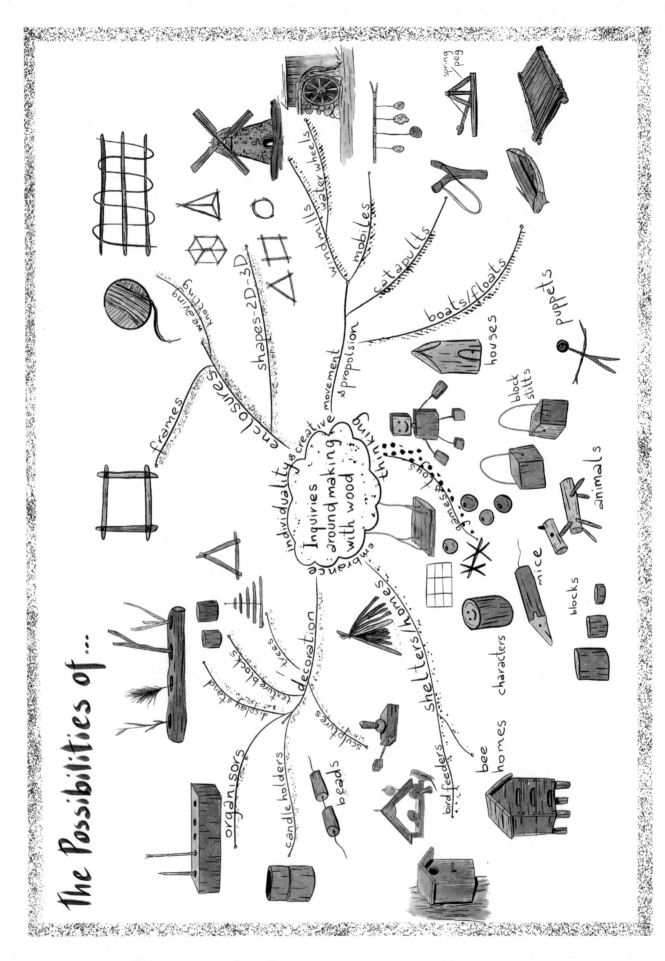

The Possibilities of...

Inquiries around making with wood

individuality & creative
thinking
embrace
organisors
candle holders
beads
sculptures
display stand
texture blocks
trees
decoration
shelters/homes
bird feeders
bee homes
characters
mice
blocks
animals
games & toys
block stilts
houses
puppets
boats/floats
catapults
mobiles
water wheels
windmills
movement & propulsion
shapes-2D-3D
weaving
knotting
enclosures
frames
spring peg

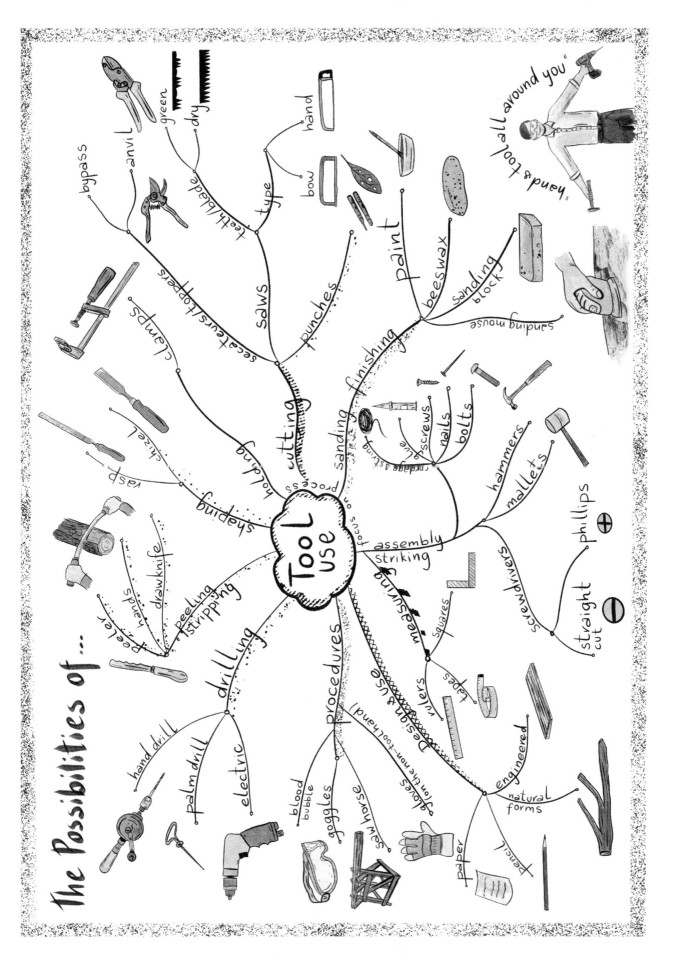

The Possibilities of...

Tool Use

"hands tool all around you"

process

cutting
sanding
finishing
assembly
striking
measuring
Design & use
procedures
drilling
shaping
holding

saws
- type
  - hand
  - bow
- teeth/blade
  - dry
  - green
secateurs/loppers
- bypass
- anvil
clamps
chisel
rasp
spoke
drawknife
peeler
peeling/stripping

punches
paint
beeswax
sanding block
sanding mouse
cordage & string
glue
screws
nails
bolts
hammers
mallets
screwdrivers
- straight cut
- phillips
squares
rulers
tape
(on the non-tool hand)
gloves
goggles
saw horse
(hand)
paper
pencil
engineered
natural forms

hand drill
palm drill
electric

Summary Mind Maps - The Learning Journey

The reality is that to be responsive, you may not reach all the ideas that you can list or that children share with you. That is okay; it just means that you are in a creative space. The way we can show the reality of what experiences and opportunities actually took place are noted at the back of the Floorbook®. The adult draws a summary mind map (usually without pictures) of what actually happened in the inquiry. This is called the Learning Journey.

The summary mind map is then used to note down the Floorbook® page where the evidence is documented of what happened in your program and will support visitors such as family members or quality assurance officers.

Compiling the Learning Journey as you go through the inquiry gives an overview of the curriculum but also the flexibility to be more child-centered in your practice.

The journal pages in this section are designed for you to note what the children in your space enjoy doing. This ensures that planning is place-based and connects to the culture and community you work in.

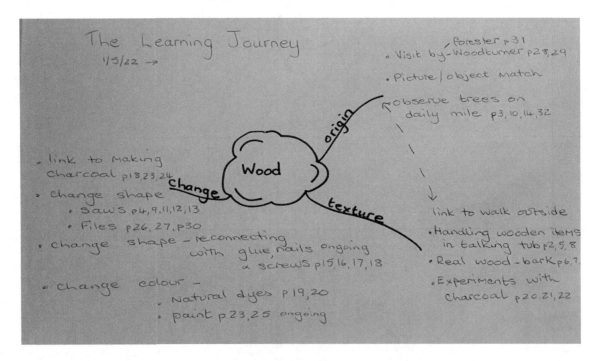

Journal Prompt

These pages are for you to organize the ideas that children share about working with wood over the years. They can be used to stimulate conversations with all the children over the years you work.

Use these blank mind map pages to note down children's ideas and theories of what they like exploring about wood. Following pages include some examples from previous groups of children.

Copy these pages or download a printable version from
www.mindstretchers.academy/series-downloads

Journal Prompt

Line of Inquiry	Activity / Experience
Knowledge of types of wood and bark	Bending and breaking of green and dead wood
	Compare pine, oak, and other varieties of wood for working and whittling
	Research into soft and hardwoods
	Use of randomized offcuts of wood in an outdoor construction area to extend the more structured block play area inside
Creation of artifacts	Encourage the use of woodworking skills to produce creative artifacts with the use of additional resources such as wire, string, leaves, bark, and feathers
	Creation of a wood workshop to offer a range of natural and manufactured wood; tools and work horse
	Use of found wood is balanced with leaving wood for animals
Design and creation of equipment/implements	Design and creation of implements such as rules, frames, cutlery, and cooking sticks develop simple whittling skills
	Use pictures of wooden spoons, forks, knives, picture frames, rulers, and stirrers to support this
	Provide different oils and conduct experiments to determine which solutions help preserve wood once shaped
	Teach skills to make objects such as bat boxes and birdhouses
	Application of the skills to new projects
Whittling as a tool for creating writing implements	Use whittling skills to sharpen ends of wood used as pencils for dipping into various inks and solutions
	Use this as a motivational stimulus for creating functional writing such as a "how to" guide or anecdotal writing such as poetry about whittling
Children's awareness and management of risk	Encourage children to create their own risk assessment written by themselves or scribed on their behalf
	Encourage children to explore the outdoor area for suitable wood - if there are no surrounding trees, the task could be looking in their garden or local park for suitable wood
	Encourage children to use their new skills to help peel vegetables and fruit for a snack
	Organize a whittling activity where children organize and develop their space - step back and observe the engagement and wellbeing

Historical use of wood work as a skill	Provide examples from different countries of whittling skills and products, from utensils to sculptures
	Find out about deforestation and afforestation
	Join or start a tree planting project or conservation activity to encourage a contribution for future generations

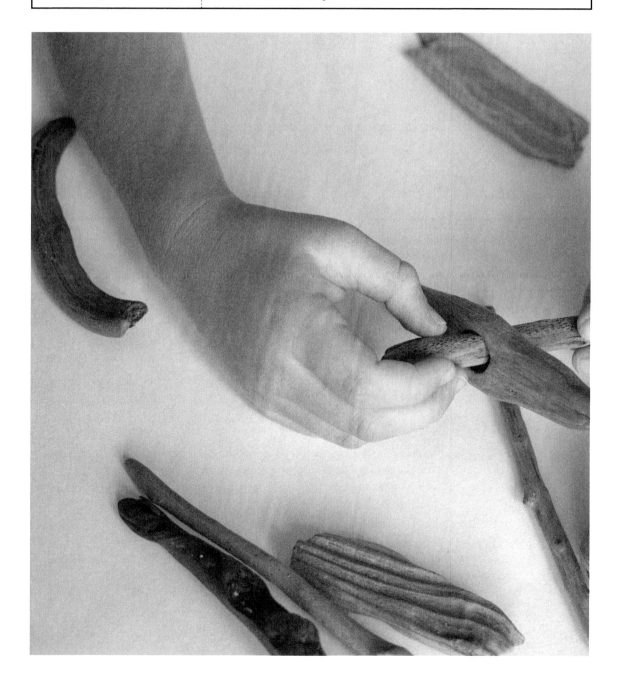

Journal Prompt

What lines of inquiry could come from these images?

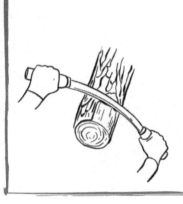

How will you continue to balance challenge and repetition in your program?

Spring Wood

Sapwood

Summer Wood

Pith

Inner Bark

Heartwood

Outer Bark

Cambium Layer

3
Curricular Links

As noted earlier, there are two ways to approach curriculum design and planning:

- One is to offer opportunities that are real world inquiries as shared within the Planning Possibilities chapter. These contextual moments are then tracked back to a set of national curriculum experiences and outcomes.
- The other is through the teaching of discrete subjects often referred to as curriculum-led.

Each section in this chapter provides the Line of Inquiry and the experiential opportunities to explore it. The journal pages are organized into curricular subjects as a guide to your planning.

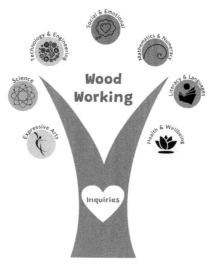

Area of Inquiry

1. Knowledge of types of wood and bark
2. Different materials for wood marking

Area of Inquiry

1. Creation of artifacts (Case Study 1 & 2)
2. Use of wood and bark shavings for creativity

Area of Inquiry

1. Design and creation of equipment/implements (Case Study 1)
2. Development of technology in whittling use
3. Methods for preserving wood

Area of Inquiry

1. Promoting mathematical concepts such as measurement, shape and time (Case Study 1)

Area of Inquiry

1. Whittling as a tool for creating writing implements (Case Study 1 & 2)
2. Opportunities for functional/anecdotal writing

Area of Inquiry

1. Children's awareness and management of risk (Case Study 1 & 2)
2. Active outdoor learning experiences (Case Study 1 & 2)
3. Whittling as an activity to promote well being and concentration (Case Study 1 & 2)
4. Use of whittling skills in food preparation

Area of Inquiry

1. Historical use of whittling as a skill
2. Natural resources in the environment (Case Study 2)

Science

Area of Inquiry Concept / Knowledge / Skill	Opportunities for Experiential Learning Experiences
1. Conceptual knowledge of types of wood and bark	
When wood is freshly cut, it is easy to bend because it contains water (sap). This also makes whittling bark very easy as it comes straight off.	Provide pupils with a selection of freshly cut green branches and dead sticks and encourage them to try bending or breaking them to explore the different properties of each. This can be used as a starting point to discuss why sticks have such different characteristics.
Certain trees, such as oak and beech, are called hardwoods, whereas other trees, such as pine and larch, are considered softwood. Hardwood is generally harder to work with than softwoods.	Cut some small pine and oak branches and allow pupils to whittle them to see if they can notice any differences when working with the wood. This experience could then form the basis for a research investigation into soft and hardwoods.
2. Different materials for wood marking	
You can effectively mark and draw on wood using pens, lead pencils, charcoal, and some natural paints.	Support pupils to whittle the bark from a fresh stick and then encourage them to decorate or mark using a material or solution of their choosing. Offer pupils a range of materials that can be used for marking and investigate which one works the best.
Pyrography is a traditional method that uses heat to mark wood.	Research the traditional method of pyrography and look at the range of different artworks and pieces that have been created using this technique.

Dr. Claire Warden

Science

Area of Inquiry Concept / Knowledge / Skill	Opportunities for Experiential Learning Experiences
1.	
2.	

Expressive Arts

Area of Inquiry Concept / Knowledge / Skill	Opportunities for Experiential Learning Experiences
1. Creation of artifacts	
Whittling, sawing, sanding, and chiseling are all ways to change the appearance of wood.	Allow the children freedom to use their whittling skills to produce a range of creative artifacts, from whittling the bark of a stick to make it look like a tree to delicately shaping the end of a stick into a bird shape. A range of additional resources, such as string, wire, leaves, bark, should be offered as part of continuous provision to develop their ideas.
2. Using byproducts to aid sustainable practices	
The shavings of wood and bark can be used as a resource for a wide range of different purposes.	Once the children have whittled, encourage them to be as creative as they can with the bark shavings and to see what they can make. The bark can work excellently as hair or clothes for small world scenarios.
Wood and bark shaving provide a rich sensorial material to explore smell, texture, and appearance.	Work with the children to explore wood shavings as a material and encourage them to describe their different experiences with it. Due to its range of sensorial properties, this will provide a rich stimulation for language.

Expressive Arts

Area of Inquiry Concept / Knowledge / Skill	Opportunities for Experiential Learning Experiences
1.	
2	

Technology & Engineering

Area of Inquiry Concept / Knowledge / Skill	Opportunities for Experiential Learning Experiences
1. Research, design, and creation skills	
Implements such as rulers, frames, cutlery, and cooking sticks can be made using simple whittling techniques.	Encourage the children to make their own utensils using their whittling skills. The children could be shown pictures of wooden items to share some of the possibilities (e.g. spoons, forks, knives, picture frames, rulers, and stirrers) and be supported to make tools like them.
2. Development of technology and wood	
Humans have used wood in a variety of ways over time.	Children can be given the opportunity to research the ways that people throughout history have used machines and resources to produce charcoal. Small rates of production using a small kiln can be compared to mass production in industry.
3. Methods for preserving wood	
A range of different solutions such as olive, walnut, linseed, and vegetable oil can be used to help preserve wood once it has been whittled.	Provide the children with a range of different oils and conduct an experiment to determine which ones preserve the wood the most effectively. The focus could be on color, smell, texture, and appearance.

Dr. Claire Warden

Technology & Engineering

Area of Inquiry Concept / Knowledge / Skill	Opportunities for Experiential Learning Experiences
1.	
2.	

Mathematics & Numeracy

Area of Inquiry Concept / Knowledge / Skill	Opportunities for Experiential Learning Experiences
1. Recording mathematical thinking	
The use of whittled pens and homemade inks can be used to help motivate children to engage with math.	Support the children to use their homemade inks and whittled pens to record their mathematical thinking on a range of different surfaces in both the indoor and outdoor environment.
2. Promoting mathematical concepts such as measurement, shape, and time	
Math has a purpose in design.	Encourage the children to design the artifacts and utensils that they will make using the whittling skills, ensuring that they focus on detailing measurements and exact recordings of their ideas. During the process of making the utensils, encourage the children to use their mathematical skills to measure out the wood and to think about the shapes involved in making their product.

Mathematics & Numeracy

Area of Inquiry Concept / Knowledge / Skill	Opportunities for Experiential Learning Experiences
1.	
2.	

Area of Inquiry Concept / Knowledge / Skill	Opportunities of Experiential Learning Experiences
1. Whittling as a tool for making writing implements	
Writing materials can be made by whittling.	Whittling skills can be used to sharpen the ends of wood which can then be used as pencils or pens for dipping in different kinds of inks and solutions. These pens can then be experimented with on a range of different surfaces such as paper, wood, and different materials.
2. Opportunities for functional and anecdotal writing	
Wood working can inspire us to write and draw.	The process of whittling can be a motivating stimulus for creating functional writing. For example, pupils can be encouraged to write safety procedures or "How to" Guides. Pupils could also be encouraged to use the experience of whittling for anecdotal writing, such as constructing poetry about why they like whittling. Slices of varnished wood can provide a surface for use with whiteboard markers rather than paper. Create discs of wood with numbers, images, and shapes to use inside and outside.

Dr. Claire Warden

Area of Inquiry Concept / Knowledge / Skill	Opportunities for Experiential Learning Experiences
1.	
2.	

Health & Wellbeing

Area of Inquiry Concept / Knowledge / Skill	Opportunities for Experiential Learning Experiences
1.Children's awareness and management of risk	
Children are able to assess self-risk, and the more we can trust them to make decisions and provide supportive environments for them to do so, the more they will thrive.	Children can be supported to create their own Benefit Risk Assessment about woodworking. This will encourage them to make decisions about how to look after themselves and others. This risk assessment can be written down by children or recorded from their words by an adult. Display their guidelines and procedures in the wood working area.
2. Active outdoor learning experiences	
Handling wood is an activity that is very appropriate for taking outside.	Children can be encouraged to explore the outdoor area and look for wood that might be suitable for using in their projects. If there are no trees in the area, they could be given the task of searching for trees in their garden or local park and finding out if they would be suitable for whittling.
3. Whittling as an activity to promote well being and concentration	
Whittling is considered by many people as an activity that is therapeutic.	Organize a whittling activity where the children are given a sense of space and freedom so that they have the opportunity to engage fully with their whittling activity. Ensuring that correct supervision and safety coaching has taken place prior to this activity will ensure that the activity is relatively low risk. When doing this activity, encourage the teacher to step back and observe the engagement and wellbeing levels of the children.
4. Use of whittling skills in food preparation	
The same whittling technique used with Lancashire peelers can be used for peeling fruit and vegetables.	Encourage children to use their whittling skills to help peel fruit and vegetables which could be eaten for snack or lunch.

Area of Inquiry Concept / Knowledge / Skill	Opportunities for Experiential Learning Experiences
1.	
2.	

Social & Emotional

Area of Inquiry Concept / Knowledge / Skill	Opportunities for Experiential Learning Experiences
1. Historical use of whittling by humans	
Whittling and wood carving has been used by a variety of different people and communities throughout history in the areas of art, religion, industry, and recreation.	Give the children a research task to find out as much as they can about whittling and woodcarving on the internet. They will find different examples from country folk whittling spoons and bowls to wood sculptures in cathedrals.
2. Natural resources in the environment	
Wood can be a sustainable energy resource if it is used sensibly and we plant and look after the trees in the environment.	Research why using wood in sensible quantities can make it a sustainable resource. The children could find out about deforestation and afforestation.
Softwoods are the main source of wood used for timber products.	The use of wood as a resource could start a tree planting project or a conservation activity within the school which could help raise the children's contribution to their local school environment and allow them to make a contribution to future generations.

Social & Emotional

Area of Inquiry Concept / Knowledge / Skill	Opportunities for Experiential Learning Experiences
1.	
2.	

4

Daily Planning

O ur role is to enable children to take control of some of their learning. An inquiry-based approach is a child-centered teaching strategy that enables children to follow their interests and fascinations while developing independence, knowledge, and thinking skills. We are still intentional as adults and have a skill level that allows us to respond in the moment, but we are also able to analyze and plan to keep our interactions authentic, our spaces enticing, and our experiences engaging.

Planning needs to be responsive as it is adapted to the weather, group dynamic of the children, unexpected opportunities, and staffing. Although there is always some intent in the experiences and opportunities we engage with, the exact outcome will be different for every child. It is this child-centered nature of education that makes it so effective. As the experiences have some planning behind them, it cannot be described as pure play, which, by its very nature, is spontaneous and unplanned.

There are a number of ways to think about how you structure the experiences and how your interactions give clear messages about your level of expectation.

Directions

This is the process of stating what will happen. It may sound like this: "John and Lara, go to the woodworking area. Today, you will make a picture frame using 4 sticks in a square." This is seen as adult-directed as children have no choice about the space, time, resources, and what they may do. The adult has removed a large degree of agency.

Invitations

This gives clear expectations and intent. In many cases, it is not something children can choose *not* to do. It may sound like this: "In the woodworking area, there is wood cut to length, as well as string and wire. See if you can make a square frame and show me what you made by the end of the day."

Provocations

This style of interaction is consultative. Conversation and debate are triggered through the use of a question, event, picture, or object in meetings whether as a group or in dialogue. The Floorbooks® are used to record children's ideas and theories which are then taken from there and transferred into the daily planning grid to add more operational detail for the staff team.

The planning journal is the place where the operational notes are recorded for everyone to access. They are designed to be completed by the staff team so that planning is completed by people with multiple perspectives of the children and their actions/words. Inquiry-based pedagogies are applicable to one-to-one situations and groups of children in settings; they work across all the locations of inside, outside, and beyond. It is a mindset that supports you as the adult to value and appreciate the complex embedded knowledge that children already have and, in turn, motivates you to work with them so that children are trusted to seek out information for themselves and empowered to find out more about what interests them.

Elements are included to link to the inquiry-based approach in the Floorbooks®. This will ensure that the team using this book consider the Floorbook® and the Planning Journal as part of the same pedagogical approach.

This section explains the purpose of the sections that are provided as an overview.

 ## Line of Inquiry

As explained in the planning possibilities chapter, if the whole team is aware of children's underlying fascinations, their interactions and planning for spaces and experiences can explore them further.

 ## Possible Line of Development (P.L.O.D)

Linked to the content of the Floorbook®, possible lines of development are written as a next step. There is a tendency to write down activities on planning sheets. For example, if we wrote that the next step was to "go outside on a windy day", it doesn't convey why the experience or opportunity is taking place. It could be that it links to an outcome in the curriculum or a child's idea. So, it could be:

- "Go to collect bark in order to talk about texture"; or

- "Introduce squared paper to the woodworking area to support ideas around area."

The documentation of the playful experiences would then go back into the Floorbook® through the photos and words you note down.

Focus

Planning journals are designed to improve practice and include supporting adult interactions. They make the invisible thinking more visible, which is beneficial to new staff. Writing down a specific thing to have in mind supports adults to consider their interaction within the experience alongside their general support and care of children. If the P.L.O.D. is "collect sticks to explore length," what will the adult be doing? Will the adult be giving affirmation and a sense of permission to play? What language could they use beyond shorter and longer?

Link

When adults and children make links between different areas of learning or links between an experience at home and in the setting, it helps them to learn.

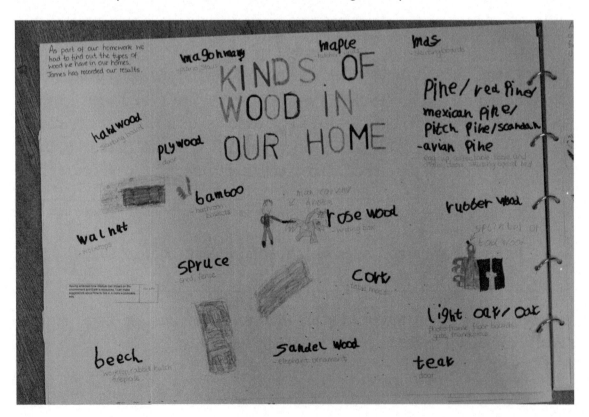

Focusing on inside, outside, and beyond is written about elsewhere (*Learning With Nature*, Warden 2015), but let us just consider how encounters with wood are different across three locations and how we can be mindful of this when we make links in our planning.

Inside	Outside	Beyond
• Create natural wood areas in more rigid construction areas • Plant a tree inside • Take things off windows so that children can see the trees outside • Use wood when setting up small world areas • Put up frames with images of trees and wood or objects made from wood • Create a Talking Tub of images and objects connected to wood • Increase the amount of sustainably sourced wooden resources • Create a woodworking area with tool board/carpet surface for sound deadening and smaller items of wood	• Plant a tree (in a large pot if necessary) and set up routines for watering in dry weather • Work with upcycled wood such as pallets to make furniture for something like a mud kitchen • Be aware of the trees and roots when outside • Take time to be under a tree • Create a stick zone • Design a transient art area with containers of loose parts such as sticks, bark, leaves, and seed pods • Use stumps of wood for seating • Create a woodworking area with larger pieces of wood	• Awareness of trees and forests nearby • Regular visits to trees to notice changes over time • Take collecting bags on walks to gather a range of local sticks, leaves etc. • Contact local building yards/ sawmill for wood offcuts • Create a large scale art area which children define and use

 Engage

The younger the child, the more intuitive and responsive the adult needs to be as the child responds to the world around them. All children deserve to be with adults who consider how they will offer an experience or an opportunity. When we offer a play provocation, we can do it beautifully and carefully or not. Being nature-based does not equate to not being careful and thoughtful about what we do and how we create our environments. Children learn from observing adults, and the care you take of the natural world and the resources it shares with us. In this section of the daily planning, we note as a team how we will engage the children. An example may be standing outside and talking about trees to draw attention to them, or it could be collecting your own bark in a basket rather than watching children do it and you supervise. It could also be that a giant branch appears in the room first thing in the morning as a provocation for an inquiry into changing wood.

The process of reflection is ongoing. Adults do it all the time and more so when you are working in a nature-based way. Many team members have individual reflective journals that they complete as part of their continual professional development. This section is different to those as it is targeted towards quality improvement as a team as we build rich, stimulating environments for playful inquiries.

The planning cycle includes a process of reviewing what happened so that we continually learn. After the intentional experiences are finished, the planning sheet asks you to consider three things before you consider what to do next.

 Investigate

We always need to be open to the idea that children will bring something new to the experience. In an emergent curriculum, no two days are the same. This exciting way to plan allows both childrens and adult ideas to come forward. Consider these questions:

- How did the children respond?

- What do they want to learn more about?

Using the term "I wonder" allows children space to think and contribute using phrases, such as "I wonder… What is it? How could I use my tools to whittle it? Where shall we go to get what we need to make a frame out of sticks? How can we use it? What could we change to make it better?"

 Documentation

Documentation can be done through what children do, say, make, and write. As noted in the planning possibilities chapter, think about who you are documenting.

Make observation notes in this section of what children did. Were there new words? A moment of wonder? Make a note of where the images taken today should go. Is there an individual learning story or perhaps images taken for the Floorbook®?

 Reflect

Planning is about improving the experiences and opportunities you offer at set points in the day and being organized to respond to children and their pure play through continuous provision. Not every day is perfect, and sometimes it is good to take the time to record here if there were challenges about the opportunities you offered.

 P.L.O.D.s

The next group of P.L.O.D.s can be taken directly from the Floorbook®, or they may just come from the unplanned conversations and observations. Writing those down in your daily planning means that the planning coordinator can read the sheets and take children's ideas forward.

Journal Prompt

These pages are for the operational notes on what will happen every day in your program. They link to the Lines of Inquiry and the Possible Lines of Development (P.L.O.D.) that you have gathered from the Floorbook® and general observations of the children.

WEEKLY OVERVIEW

MONDAY	TUESDAY	WEDNESDAY

THURSDAY	FRIDAY	NOTES

REMINDERS

_____   _____

_____   _____

_____   _____

Line of Inquiry -

What is the broad underlying main idea in this experience?

P.L.O.D. -

What are you planning to do and why? Ask yourself "So what?" each time you note down an activity to monitor if it has meaning and connection to children.

Focus -

What is the intentional focus of planned experience? It could be an area of curriculum such as numbers to 10, the use of vocabulary, engagement of key children, muscle control, or joy.

Link -

How are you relating this to children's previous learning? How can children create a connection between home and these experiences in setting?

Engage -

How will you engage children? What resources do you need to get ready? Where will you offer the provocation/invitation?

After the experience fill these areas in.

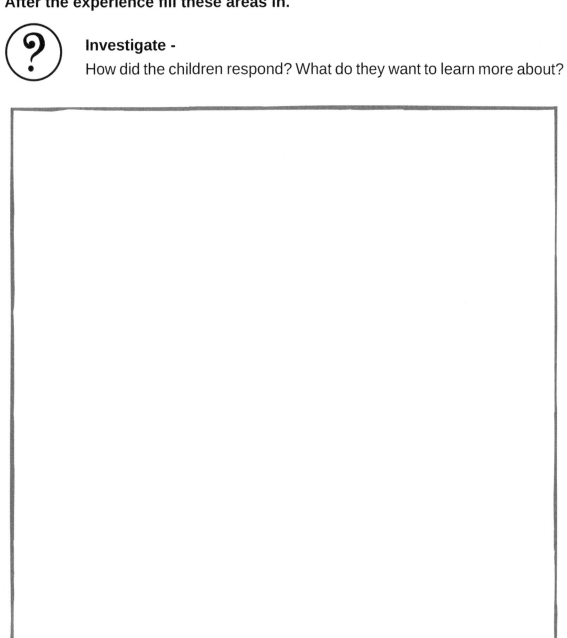

Investigate -

How did the children respond? What do they want to learn more about?

Documentation -

What did children actually do, say, make, and write? Is it going in the Floorbook®, individual portfolios, or on display?

Reflect -

How did it go for you and the children? What changes would you make if you did it again?

Next P.L.O.D. -

What is the next step in the learning journey for these children?

Use this page to reflect on the impact of your planning on the quality of experience that children have.

Things to keep the same.

Things to change.

NOTES:

_____

_____

_____

_____

_____

_____

5
Case Studies with Analysis and Possible Lines of Development

As part of this philosophy, we encourage children to be involved in documentation. The images taken in this chapter include those by the adult and the child.

These images would be printed out and used within the Floorbook®. In the morning of each day, children are encouraged to cut out and stick in the photographs they think are most important. On occasion where the learning is significant, the entire case study is shared in the Family Book as evidence of individual engagement.

Case Study 1: Consulting with Children with a 3D Mind Map

A group of 2-4 year old children showed an interest in whittling at the nursery. The staff consulted them using the 3D Mind Map with a Talking Tub to promote a sharing and exploration of the children's knowledge about wood and whittling. At the beginning of the process, the practitioner put three Lancashire peelers in the middle as a provocation for discussion. The practitioner then opened up the discussion by asking if anyone knew what the tools were used for. One of the children responded by saying, "Peeling potatoes," which then sparked other contributions about peeling fruit and vegetables. When the children spoke, their contributions were recorded on the yellow strips of paper and were put down in front of them. When one of the children mentioned peeling trees, small pieces of wood were added to the tools to stimulate discussion about this topic.

As the children explored the objects, their discussion levels increased. When they began talking about peeling the bark, a small bag of bark peelings were introduced for them to explore. "Like that," responded one of the children.

When the peelings were shared across the children, they began to explore them and described what they were like. As the children explored the objects, their discussion levels increased. When they began talking about peeling the bark, a small bag of bark peelings were introduced for them to explore.

"It's curly, curly for the nest for the birds," one girl stated.

One of the older boys then commented that, "They're supposed to protect the trees."

When the session came to an end, several of the children stayed to explore the bark shavings further. One of the young girls began to wrap the bark peelings around one of the sticks and then used the peelings to make a transient picture, stating that "It's a snail."

Following the session, the practitioner arranged all the contributions made by the children into lines of inquiry to help organize the concepts so that they could be linked to form P.L.O.D.s. From their contributions, it became clear that the children were particularly interested in exploring the texture and appearance of the bark peelings and were able to link their thinking to knowledge about peeling vegetables.

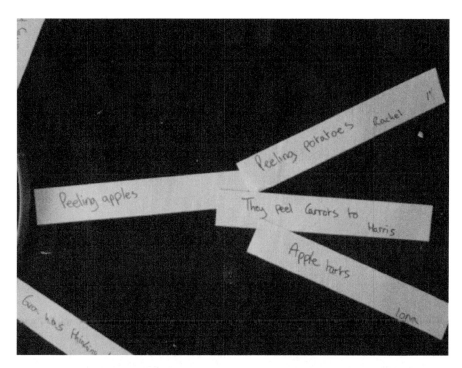

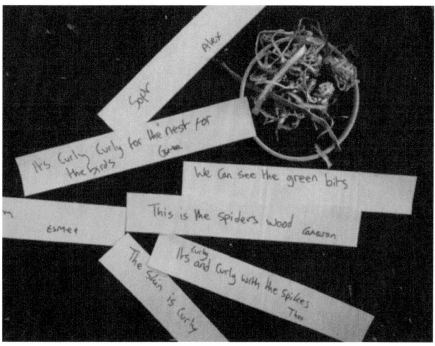

Analysis of Learning

The 3D Mind Mapping session revealed key aspects of embedded knowledge around curls in hair, peeling apples, and spirals in snail shells.

P.L.O.D.s

1. Explore different kinds of bark to focus on texture, appearance and smell.
2. Offer simple whittling activities, including wood and root vegetables, to allow the children to revisit the basic safety procedures when whittling.
3. Collect and use wood shavings from the plane and use them in creative areas.
4. Search for snails and explore the similarity and differences across shells.

Case Study 2: Whittling Wood (2-6 years)

1. Making Stick People

During an afternoon session in our outdoor area, we found some fallen branches, and the children began to explore them. Using their whittling skills, they shaved off the outer bark from the sticks they had found. It was suggested by a member of staff that they try to make stick men out of the branches.

Two of the older boys took time as they gradually whittled the ends of the branch, and when asked what they were doing, one of them revealed that, "I am whittling my stick man some hands."

Another of the boys decided to whittle the whole stick saying that he "needs to have smooth skin."

Once they had whittled their sticks, the children used different lengths of wire, string, and pine cones to add features to their stick men. One of the young boys used a pine cone as a head while another wrapped wire around small bracken leaves to make hair on top of the stick man's whittled face. One of the older boys spent time adding detail to the face of one of the stick men and, with some help from the staff, was able to create a detailed face. When he was happy with the face, he used some leftover charcoal from the fire to color his eyes and mouth.

When the children had created their stick men, they used him in a creative role play scenario. One of the older boys put him up a tree saying that:

"He likes climbing the trees,"

Meanwhile, a small group of children started to create a stickman home using natural materials found in the transient art area. When they had made two different houses - one from bark and grass and the other from wooden logs - they used the environment as a role play area, giving the stick men names and jobs to do in the home environment.

Analysis of Learning

As well as the learning benefits of whittling discussed in Case Study 1, the pupils in this scenario are able to express their creative abilities with wood. One of the boys engaged highly as he finely sculpted the hands and face of his stick man using his pen knife. The use of the pine cone as a head, as well as the entrapment of different natural materials using wire, shows both a high level of manual dexterity and creativity in the design of the stick man features. The progression to the design and building of the stick man houses highlights further creativity with the natural materials and emphasizes the value of the stick people as a provocation for role play and storytelling opportunities.

P.L.O.D.s

1. Develop creation of stick people stories using the whittled stick men as motivations for storytelling/writing.
2. Create accessories for the stick man figures and use them to stimulate further creative language opportunities linked to role play and small world moments.
3. Provide opportunities for decorating the candle holders using natural paints, charcoal, or calligraphy to encourage creative expression.

2. Making Pencils

During a morning session outside, the children used their whittling skills to make pencils. Along with a member of staff, they collected fresh branches from a fallen tree and then began to whittle away the ends of their sticks. When asked why she was whittling the sticks, one of the young girls explained that:

"It has to be sharp, and that's what whittling does."

When asked further why the stick needed to be sharp, the girl responded saying that:

"It won't work if the pencil isn't sharp; we need it to be pointy."

When the children were happy with their pencils, they used mud ink to write with and found big pieces of wood and bark to write on. After testing out the pencils, several of the children went back to the work bench to further develop their pencils. One of the girls, aged 5 years, used wire to wrap around the pencil to work as a handle. Another of the children decided to gently whittle the top of the pencil and leave the shavings feathering from the pencil exclaiming that it made it look "leafy."

They then went back to writing with the pencils with the mud ink. This time, however, the children began to experiment with different surfaces.

They tried out a range of different pieces of wood to see which would work best.

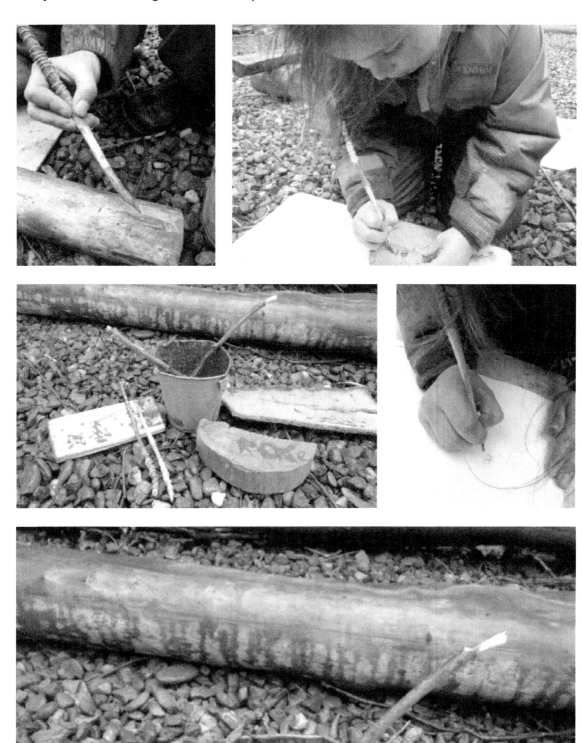

After experimenting on a rounded tree stump, one of the young girls asked for paper and then began writing once more. She spent time trying to write more delicately so that the lines of her writing were thinner.

She then manipulated the tip of the pencil and pushed back the fibers so that the pencil remained thin and pointy. When it became too blunt, she intermittently returned to the tool bench and whittled the end until it was sharp again.

One of the boys who had not taken part in the first part of the investigation came to look at the objects. When he realized that he could write with them, he took the mud ink and pencils inside the kindergarten kitchen and used them to write in the

Floorbook®. When parents arrived, he explained to some of them how the mud ink and pencils worked saying that,

"You just dip it in and write like this: dip, dip, dip."

Several of the parents then signed their names in the Floorbook® as they collected their children.

Analysis of Learning

The children showed an understanding of the need for their pencils to be thin in order to write properly with them, which is something they are able to achieve by the use of their whittling skills. When the young girl whittled her stick again once it had become too soft, it underlined her ability to maintain the dimensions of the pencil. Several of the children were able to express their creativity with their whittling skills by whittling the tops of the pencil and leaving parts of the peeled bark attached to the wood. The exploration of using mud as an ink shows resourcefulness, and the time spent mixing the mud together highlights their knowledge of mixing solutions to create suspensions. Several of the children write on different pieces of wood before settling on the use of paper, highlighting a use of experimentation and perseverance with the activity. The application of the whittled pencils for writing with the mud ink provides an example of ways of engaging the children with literacy, and the success of the children in writing their names highlights this. Parents and carers took these skills and fed back that they had made more "pencils" at home and made other types of "inks."

P.L.O.D.s

1. Experiment further with different types of materials for writing such as chalk, water, natural paints, and charcoal to explore writing skills.
2. Make pencils using different types of wood to determine the differences between soft and hardwoods and different species of tree.

Case Study 3: Whittling Wood (7-8 years)

1. Making Measuring Sticks

During an outdoor learning session in the local woodland, the school class explored their current interest in numbers and measurement. The class already had several woodland sessions where they had learned the skills for sawing and whittling safely. The class was given pieces of fresh wood and access to a variety of tools in order to create a measuring stick. The pupils began by whittling their sticks using a potato peeler.

When the children had whittled all of the bark from their stick, they used a measuring tape to determine where they should mark out the measurements on their own stick, and it was decided to use centimeters as the unit of measurement on the stick. Several of the children used a pencil to mark on the whittled wood while others used paint pens. During a discussion about this, one of the children commented that "I'm going to use a pencil 'cos it won't rub off." The children experimented with different ways of marking accurately; some worked with a partner who held the measuring tape in place while others put both the measuring tape and stick on the ground and matched them up.

  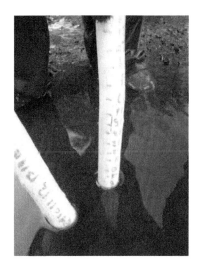

When they had finished marking the numbers, the children marked their initials on the bottom of the stick and laid them out to dry on the ground. Due to so much rainy weather over the past few days, it was suggested that the children use their new measuring sticks to measure the different depths of the many puddles on the path. The children first estimated how deep they were and then used their sticks to work out the depth.

Analysis of Learning

The experience of whittling in itself provides a variety of learning benefits. In each scenario, the pupils were able to explore the properties of wood as they gently peeled the layers of bark back and felt the existence of sap that creates the soft, almost buttery feel to the wood. In scenario one, for example, several pupils spent up to thirty minutes whittling their pieces of wood, showing a particularly high level of engagement and apparent similar level of wellbeing. Moreover, the practical application of the pupil's awareness of risk is important, and we can see that the pupils have learned how to correctly whittle in order to keep themselves and others safe. This is surmised when one of the pupils described that "whittling is a skill that needs great concentration in case you cut anyone by accident."

Bringing the very practical activity of whittling together with the use of number and measurement allows mathematical understanding to be applied within a context, which can often help to make the learning more motivational for pupils.

P.L.O.D.s

1. Experiment with different ways to mark wood such as marker pens, pencils, paint, charcoal, and pyrography and choose which tool is the most effective.
2. Investigate the different layers of bark on trees, focusing on the differences between inner and outer bark and what both trees and people use them for.
3. Provide further opportunities for measuring natural elements, such as puddles in the local environment. Support pupils to collect and record their results and interpret them appropriately.

2. Making Photo Frames

During a session in the woods, the class used their whittling skills to make a photo frame. As part of the management plan for the wood, it was decided to bring in a selection of fresh wood harvested in advance by the session leader. The pupils found appropriate areas to begin their whittling activity, some sat on the floor, others on logs, while some sat in the hammocks. When asked about whittling, one of the pupils described that:

"I really liked doing the whittling because you get a knife and scrape all the wood off. It lets you think about all sorts. You can make it smooth if you work hard," while another commented that:

"I like it because it's easy to do but you get good looking results that you can be proud of."

When the sticks had been whittled, the children sawed the stick into four pieces. They used a measuring tape or their own wooden measure so that all the sticks were the right length to fit the shape that they wanted to create. Any remaining pieces of bark were then whittled from the individual sticks and turned into designs made into the wood. When questioned about the whittling process, one of the pupils described that "you have to push the peeler down the stick. It's green under the bark, but if you keep going it turns white." When the pupils were happy that their sticks had been whittled enough, they arranged the pieces on the woodland floor. Some pupils created squares and rectangles, while others made triangles. String was then used to tie the pieces together. Pupils used a square lash to ensure that the sticks were connected tightly. When the frames had been fixed together, the pupils created transient art inside them using the woodland materials. A group of children experimented with artworks using the frames together to make a range of sculptural forms.

Analysis of Learning

This concept was applied in a similar way through photo frame making as the pupils then progressed from whittling the wood to measuring the wood appropriately to explore shape and size. The creation of both the measuring sticks and frames provided the opportunity to explore an area of the curriculum in focus; the pupils progressed to measuring the depth of the puddles on the estate road using the measuring sticks, and the pupils progressed to creating natural art inside the frames. The progression of learning here is key, as we can see that the pupils applied their whittling skills to gain a greater depth and application.

P.L.O.D.s

1. Explore different ways for decorating frames using paints, natural materials, or markings.
2. Research ways to preserve wood and provide the opportunity for pupil experimentation with methods of preservation.
3. Introduce other types of knots which can be used when working with wood, such as whipping.

We started off whittling small branches
All enjoyed trying to take each part of
bark off the branch until they come
across a knot!

Whittling is cutting small branches
pulling the bark off with a small,
tool.

WHITTLING

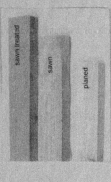
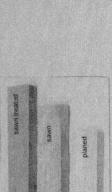

Sipo

Oregon

Abatia
Deasii

Meringue

Meabi

Afrormosia

Sapell

sawn treated

sawn

planed

Having evaluated my work, I can adapt and improve, where appropriate, through trial and error or by using feedback | TCH 1-14b TCH 2-14b

By exploring and using technologies in the wider world, I can consider its ways in which they help.

Through discovery and imagination, I can develop and use problem solving strategies to construct models. | TCH 1-14a

Whittling is good fun and relaxing to do.

It was fun and you can make cool things.
Ross

It was exciting and you can make lots of
different things. Becky

It was awesome!!! Amber

Whittling knife used to round a
corner of a piece of wood.

Safety Instructions

1. Keep a safe distance from the perso[n]
   beside you.
2. Point the blade away from you.
3. Don't touch the blade.
4. Remember a person's blood bubble.

Journal Prompt

These pages are designed for you to notice and take notes about the kinds of things that your children find fascinating about working with wood.

Journal Prompt

How effective is your setting at linking experiences inside and outside?

Journal Prompt

How do your families view woodwork?

Are there concerns you are aware of?

How will you support them to understand the value of woodwork?

Journal Prompt

Where and how do you encourage children to look back at all their adventures? Does this change if they are inside a building or outside?

6
Developing Skills

How to Run a Whittling Session

Why whittling?

We see whittling as an activity that allows children freedom, flexibility, and a chance for a lot of personal space to connect with their sense of self and their natural environment. Whittling is an activity that we use on a regular basis in our Nature Kindergartens, both during our work with teachers and as part of our project work with our Living Classrooms Charity. When we introduce whittling to a group, whether it be a small group of three year olds or a group of adults, we find that the engagement and wellbeing levels of the individuals generally increase and that the sensibility to both the environment and peers increases.

We have conducted whittling sessions where we have started the children off and simply stepped back and allowed it to continue for an hour, or even more. Sometimes, the child may use their whittling skills to make a cooking stick, a photo frame, or perhaps even a sword. Sometimes, it might just be whittling for whittling's sake as they explore the feel of shaving away the rough bark from the smooth sap wood and concentrate so much on what they are doing that the rest of the world almost stops around them. It is this type of deep level engagement that we strive for everyday in education. We are not saying that whittling will always create this, but it is absolutely an activity that can create high engagement and fascinate children and therefore, in our opinion, should be made available to children of all ages within the learning environment at school.

What to Include in a Woodwork Area

Use these images to help children organize your woodworking area and develop their vocabulary.

screws	nails	hammer
sandpaper	wood	saw
screwdriver	glue	gloves
string	wire	paint

Where to Start

When working with children in an educational environment, you will start off by whittling the bark from pieces of wood. The focus in this respect would be to ensure that the wood that the children are whittling is reasonably fresh so that they can easily shave the bark from the wood itself. Before you start with the children, it is well worth practicing yourself on a small fresh piece of wood and then an old dead bit of wood to see the difference. As you begin to integrate whittling into your practice, you will find that ensuring that the children are whittling fresh wood will help with safety as they will have more success and will not start to experiment with different techniques to get the bark away, which can often be unsafe. Another aspect to consider is the knots in wood. The knots that we find in wood are old branches that have snapped off and then slowly inverted into the wood. When children are whittling with peelers, you will find that they will struggle when they try and whittle over a knot or when they try to shave off a knot. The best thing to do here would be to either let a staff member cut it off or encourage the children to whittle around the knot.

Group Management

Whether we are working out in the woods, in the playground, or in the classroom, we will always designate a tool area where anyone wishing to whittle has to work within. This allows a staff member to keep an eye on the children with the tools.

Where to Sit

It is also important to establish an appropriate seating/kneeling room for children. A log or low bench works well as it allows children to straighten out their legs and whittle to the side of them. If there is no appropriate seating, then children are normally made to sit on one knee and whittle away to the ground. There is never an occasion where a child is allowed to whittle sitting down on with their bottom on the floor as this can open up the possibility of a child cutting their leg.

Ensuring Safety

When working with children or adults of any age, we use the concept of a "blood bubble" to help support the participants to keep themselves and each other safe. The "blood bubble" is a safe area around a child that no other person is allowed to walk in, meaning that they can use their tool without fear of cutting anyone else. The "blood bubble" is measured by the child reaching out all the way around themselves and ensuring that they cannot touch anyone.

What to Use

These 4 items will be enough to get started with woodwork and especially the process of whittling:

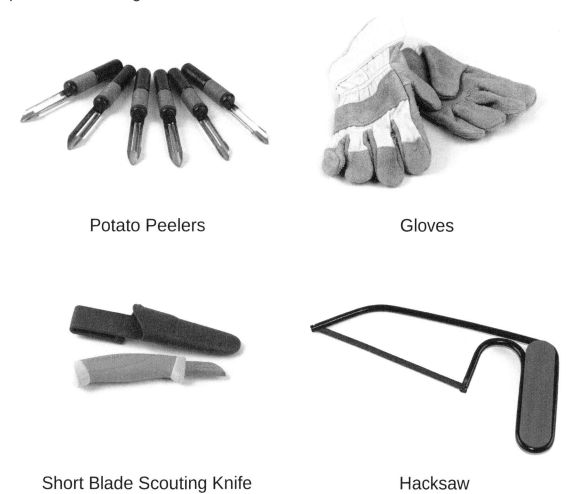

Potato Peelers   Gloves

Short Blade Scouting Knife   Hacksaw

How to Make Stick People

The joy of making stick people is to search the forest for branches and twigs that already have the hint of arms and legs coming from it. The best steps to follow are as follows:

1. Use the whittling tool of choice to shape the ends of the arms and legs. Peel off the bark to create feet and hand areas. Some people carve stripes and shapes into the "body" for clothing.

2. Run the blade around the "neck" of the person to create a line and whittle the head shape with facial features and a neck area.
3. Use charcoal to enhance the facial features.
4. Make a hole in the top to add hair made from loose materials such as shavings or twigs.

How to Make a Spoon

Birch and Sycamore are easier woods to begin with. You will need the following:

- Straight knife,

- Carving knife,

- Mallet,

- Sandpaper, and

- Oil (food grade).

1. Select a small pole about 6cm in diameter that is green and, therefore, softer to work with. Try and find one with a natural curve or slight "dog leg" that you can use as the curve of the spoon.

2. Start by cutting the pole to a little longer than you need for the finished spoon and split the pole in half, lengthways. To do this, place your knife with the edge across one end of the pole and carefully use an off cut from your pole as a mallet to knock your knife into the pole. Allow it to split slowly as forcing it at this stage may make the split run off center. Select the half that is shaped in the right way for the spoon you want to carve and whittle the split surface with your knife so that it is smooth.

3. Using a pencil, roughly draw a spoon shape onto the wood. You could use any spoon which you like the shape of as a template for this. Using the knife carefully, whittle and slice around the outline until you have completed shaping in that plane. The grain in the wood may run in different directions and dictate which way you can cut.

4. Look at your spoon from the side and decide how you would like to shape the curve of the spoon handle. If you have managed to use a pole with a natural curve or dog-leg, it may only need a little refining. Always use your knife carefully, making sure that you are always cutting away from yourself. If you have made the handle of your spoon wide in one place, you can make it thin in the other side and vice versa, shaping in this way will ensure that the spoon remains strong enough.

5. When you are satisfied with the shape of your spoon, you can turn your attention to shaping the inside of the bowl. With your hooked knife, slowly start to remove all the unwanted wood; the grain of the wood will dictate which direction you will need to cut in but, in general, cutting across the grain works well. When this is finished, you can start finishing the spoon.

If you intend to sand the spoon to a smooth finish, store it at room temperature for a few days first as this will dry the wood out a little and make sanding easier. If you intend to leave your spoon with a tooled finish, carefully go over the spoon with your knife, fine-tuning any slightly rough or uneven areas.

Finally, seal your spoon with oil. A person once said that a wooden spoon allows you to taste every meal you have ever eaten with it as a hint stays within the wood. The food grade oils will bring out the markings in the wood and also ensure it is safe for eating with.

Journal Prompt

Collect resources for new skills that could link to this fascination.

Skill 1: (e.g. Creating a wood work area)

Make a list below of supporting materials for developing this skill.
(Books, Websites, YouTube videos, Podcasts etc.)

Journal Prompt

> **Skill 2:** (e.g. Using found wood to make stick people)

Make a list below of supporting materials for developing this skill.
(Books, Websites, YouTube videos, Podcasts etc.)

Journal Prompt

Skill 3: (e.g. boxes, houses from processed wood)

Make a list below of supporting materials for developing this skill.
(Books, Websites, YouTube videos, Podcasts etc.)

_____

_____

_____

_____

_____

_____

_____

_____

_____

_____

_____

_____

_____

Journal Prompt

Skill 4:

Make a list below of supporting materials for developing this skill.
(Books, Websites, YouTube videos, Podcasts etc.)

7

Benefit Risk Assessment

The risk management process needs to balance the benefits of experience with any unseen threats that the child and adults may not be aware of. These threats are presented in the form of hazards and can be part of physical, intellectual, social, and emotional risk taking. We as adults often focus on physical hazards because they are easier to observe, but, in actual fact, the impact of emotional harm and lack of intellectual stimulation may have a great impact over a lifetime.

Benefit Risk Management

Undertake a Benefit Risk Assessment (BRA) for the site and all the activities you plan to undertake well before the experience so that you are familiar and aware of the spaces you work in and what the experience or activity entails.

Site Risk Assessment

Map the site to show emergency access in case of emergency and key features of the landscape to ensure that you know where the hazards may be on the site.

Activity Risk Assessment

The form here shows in detail some of the aspects that could cause harm. They could seem extreme for exploring wood, but one of the important aspects of this work is that safety as a broad concept needs to be in the minds of everyone involved. This is not about removing risk as we need that to learn but minimizing the hazards that may be unseen and can cause harm. Risk assessments therefore need to be accessible and read by the whole team.

Dynamic Risk Management

The weather, animal life, mood of children, skill and number of the adults you are with all play a part in the experience. There needs to be a section on any risk assessment for its adaptation to the unforeseen circumstances.

Child Voice

Children are the stakeholders in the situation, so their awareness, knowledge, and understanding of hazards should be included as a separate sheet. The Floorbook® and Talking Tub is very effective at allowing children time to understand materials and objects that, if used inappropriately, could cause harm.

Undertake a benefit risk assessment as part of the process of getting ready. Ask both adults and children the following 3 questions:

- What is good about this activity? (Benefits)

- What do we need to be careful of? (Hazards and associated Risks)

- How do we stay safe? (Precautions)

Example of Site Risk Assessment

Use an existing map of the area that shows up all the details or draw your own. Consider:

- Road access, habitat areas for animals, vegetation type, steep slopes and cliffs, bodies of water (such as rivers or lakes), and mobile reception;

- Mark the areas that you will visit and use "What Three Words" (W3W) to find the location reference;

- Mark key species of trees to visit to explore differences and similarities;

- Woodland and trees can be hazardous in strong winds. Note the refuge location and exit from site if the winds reach Force 7 (moderate gale 32-38 mph);

- Wet areas with trees as they can be unstable; and

- Direction of wind- trees develop to grow in response to a prevailing wind direction. If the wind changes it can uproot trees.

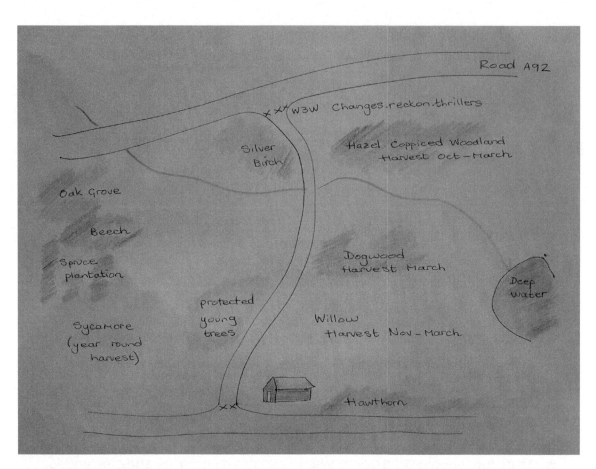

The map shows:

Road A92

xx W3W Changes.reckon.thrillers

Silver Birch

Hazel Coppiced Woodland
Harvest Oct – March

Oak Grove

Beech

Spruce plantation

Dogwood
Harvest March

Deep water

protected young trees

Willow
Harvest Nov – March

Sycamore
(year round harvest)

xx

Hawthorn

Activity Risk Assessment Example

Benefit Risk Assessment	Wood based Activities
Assessment date: 06/2011	Date for review: 09/2011 - ongoing
Assessment undertaken by:	Staff member
Approved by:	Senior staff member
Local site considerations/amendments:	Unstable tree branches, low level branches, overhang area of trees. Uneven ground conditions, or obstacles on the ground. Wood is collected from sustainable areas and done effectively without harming the tree/bush. Weather effects on ground, seating areas and other surfaces.
Benefits of whittling/wood carving:	Opportunity for children to self-risk assess Build self confidence Group cooperation Group awareness Build independence and develop trust Understanding the use of tools - creative and functional Build fine motor skills Develop woodcarving skills Develop an understanding of the properties of wood Calming and therapeutic aspects of whittling

Fascination of Earth: Wood

Hazard	Level of Risk	Precaution	Revised Risk Level
Medical conditions - respiratory issues	Medium	• Allergies and medical low respiratory issues conditions/requirements are checked prior to activity. • Participants manage their own medication or are managed by supervising adults (age appropriate).	Low
Inappropriate behavior during wood carving/ whittling activity	High	• Staff have received training in working with vulnerable groups/are Disclosure Scotland checked. • Adult ratio is appropriate and the adult is positioned appropriately to monitor children's whittling techniques and safety procedures. • Adult ratio is appropriate for supervising the rest of the group if near a designated whittling activity area. • All pupils are instructed to move and behave appropriately and with care around tool areas (e.g. use of blood bubbles). • Appropriate personal protective equipment is available and worn by participants. • Zero tolerance to inappropriate use of tools. If this occurs, tools are immediately removed from the pupil and time out from activity is given.	Low
Inappropriate use of tools	High	• Adults are trained and aware of appropriate tool handling techniques. • Wood used is selected to be appropriate to activity (e.g. willow for charcoal, larch/spruce to bend, hazel to strip, elder to create necklaces). • Teach children how to use tools and equipment correctly and use appropriate personal protective equipment. • Children are monitored and supported if necessary when carrying materials. Safe carrying and storing strategies are taught for all tools. • Creation of a whittling zone with designated seating/storage area. • Whittling - used in a seated position, drawing the knife/peeler away from the body and legs, potato peelers available on forest wrap. Adults have a knife stored in their hip belt and these are managed on a higher ratio. • All tools are monitored, treated, and stored appropriately at the end of the activity.	Low

Hazard	Level of Risk	Precaution	Revised Risk Level
Contact with sharp implements	High	● Gloves for adults and children are available to protect hands during tool use. Gloves are worn on the non-tool hand. ● Pupils are trained in the use of tools and given demonstrations and training. ● Tools are introduced progressively to pupils. Start with a Lancashire peeler and move up to a pen knife/fixed blade knife only when appropriate. ● Adults have valid first aid qualifications. ● Fresh wood is always used to begin with as it is easier to whittle. ● Pupils are encouraged to whittle around knots in wood or an adult removes knots with a knife before or during session.	Low
Cuts or injuries - from wood handling, hazardous plants, and tool handling	Medium	● Adults have appropriate first aid training. ● First aid points are established. ● First aid kits are monitored and replenished daily as appropriate. ● Cuts or injuries from wood/tool handling are cleaned and treated immediately and first aid requirements are dealt with appropriately. ● Children are monitored and supported, if necessary, when carrying materials. Safe lifting strategies are taught. ● Hazardous plants/locations must be identified in advance and contact with them prevented if appropriate.	Low

Activity Risk Assessment Template

Benefit-Risk Assessment	Wind Based Activities
Assessment date:	Date for review:
Assessment undertaken by:	
Approved by:	
Local site considerations/amendments:	
Benefits of activity:	

Hazard	Level of Risk	Precaution	Assessed Risk Level

Dynamic Risk Assessment Example

Benefit Risk Assessment	Wind Based Activities
Assessment date: 01/23	Date for review:
Assessment undertaken by: M. Morrow	Staff member
Approved by: C.H. Warden	Senior staff member
Local site Considerations/amendments:	Warm weather, dry ground, full leaf cover
Benefits of activity:	🍃 Focus on making 🍃 Development of hand and eye coordination 🍃 Social interaction (key children)

Hazard	Level of Risk	Precaution	Revised Risk Level
Inappropriate behavior	Medium	🍃 Increase the ratio of staff to children today to support the two key children staff identify. 🍃 Rituals and routines on entry to the forest area. 🍃 Clear boundaries of behavior stated and followed through.	Low
Use of tools	Medium	🍃 Children using tool wrap in a defined space. 🍃 1:3 adult child ratio to support tool use.	Low

Dynamic Risk Management Template

Our role as adults is to be risk aware. These pages are designed to be used to collate your own adjustments to the risk assessments shared. This makes them specific to your space, the weather, the children, and the skill of the adults. There should be activity (shared in this chapter), site plans, and assessments of the hazards, and dynamic risk management in place.

Benefit Risk Assessment	Wind Based Activities
Assessment date:	**Date for review:**
Assessment undertaken by:	
Approved by:	
Local site considerations/amendments:	
Benefits of activity:	

Hazard	Level of Risk	Precaution	Assessed Risk Level

Copy these pages or download a printable version from www.Mindstretchers.academy/series-downloads

Documenting the Child Voice in Risk Management

It is very important to involve the stakeholder in risk management. In this case, that is the child. Use the Talking Tub to have conversations around any hazards you are aware of. Encouraging children to draw designs and ideas as well as choosing the best location helps them be aware of space.

Writing down what they say and making reflections is part of the adult assessment, but it is recorded into the group Floorbook® so that you can all revisit it. It allows us to consider the procedures we put in place across different groups of children according to the experience rather than only their age. Understanding and embracing a fascination is at the heart of an emergent curriculum and allows us to be responsive to their inquiry into wind. Our duty of care means that we need to be aware of the implications of children's ideas and be able to risk assess any situation. Using images such as the one below allows us to raise awareness within a context that children are aware of.

Activity Child Voice Template

Use this page to gather children's ideas about how to keep themselves safe. Write on the Lines of Inquiry, issues that you feel could be discussed. Some suggestions would be sticks, deep water, strangers, high winds, fire, and use of tools.

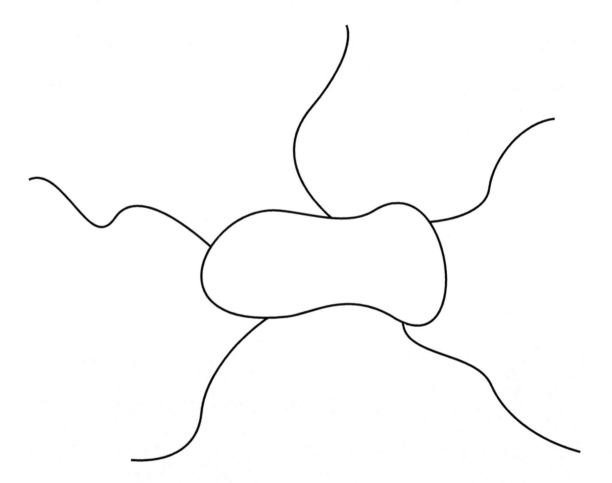

Journal Prompt

Site Risk Assessment. Use this page to draw the spaces that you intend to work with children. Urban spaces need to consider eddies and wind corridors created by buildings. Where can you walk with children to gather wood? Is there a park area away from the setting that has more trees? If traveling to a wood store to get wood, plan out how the journey itself can be part of the learning experience.

Copy these pages or download a printable version from
www.mindstretchers.academy/series-downloads

Journal Prompt

Activity Risk Assessment. Write down the benefits of going ahead with an activity from your perspective and then take note of children's thoughts. Do the benefits and hazards balance out? Could you change the type of wood to change the challenge level? Balsa is easier to use than hardwood. Narrow lengths of wood give a positive sense of success when learning to saw.

Journal Prompt

Dynamic Risk Assessment. Write down your strategies and procedures on how you will respond to changing behaviors, energy levels, and boundaries. Focus on a new area for yourself such as tool use or den building.

Copy these pages or download a printable version from
www.mindstretchers.academy/series-downloads

Journal Prompt

Child Documentation. Write down items or images to collect that you could put in the Talking Tub about wood in its widest sense. What items do you want? Who might have them?

Summary

The journey through this book has explored children's fascination with wood. Given it is very wide ranging, it could have gone in a thousand directions. I made the conscious decision to focus on the process of "making" with children, or changing the wood in some way, whether that is from sawing and sanding a block of wood or perhaps finding a stick and shaping it into a stick person.

The process of changing a piece of nature into a new form with a new purpose that may range from functional tool making to the creative process of patterning and reforming to accentuate the beauty of a piece is an enduring fascination. Children around the world are being given the opportunities to reconnect to nature through following a variety of routes. Traditional crafts and skills are part of our intergenerational knowledge. These traditions hold us together as a culture, and they acknowledge our ancestors in a living, practical way. Children show us in their play that the mastery of these skills fascinate them and the transformational process engages all aspects of their being.

This book has been created to support adults to see the benefits of working with the natural elements as a way of teaching and learning. The inclusion of curriculum concepts and skills lead to longer term developments in attitude that stay with the learner throughout their lives. We need to be able to identify and document learning outside to reinforce links across three learning environments of inside, outside, and beyond if we are to support children, families, and educational groups to "be" outside in nature. If you are enjoying this book, I would suggest you explore the other titles in the series that are, Fire, Earth, Water, and Air.

With kind regards,

Claire

www.mindstretchers.academy

About the Author

D r. Claire Warden is an international education consultant, researcher, advisor, and author. She is the founder of the multiple award winning Auchlone Nature Kindergarten and Mindstretchers Academy which are both based In Scotland, U.K.

Dr. Claire Warden is an educational consultant who has developed her approach to Nature Pedagogy and experiential learning through working in a variety of settings, including her own multi award-winning Auchlone Nature Kindergarten, advisory work, and lecturing in further education. Claire is currently based in Scotland, but she frequently travels to Australia, the United States, and elsewhere. Her unique contribution to the field of education has been recognized through many awards, and she holds her Doctorate in the "Creation and theorisation of Nature Pedagogy".

Claire is an author of over 20 books relating to early years methodology. Claire's book, *Learning with Nature – Embedding Outdoor Practice*, was well received and has gained a place as required reading on many academic education courses. In her book *Nature Kindergartens and Forest Schools*, Claire explores children's connection to nature and naturalistic spaces such as forest schools, forest kinder-gartens, woodland camps, and nature kindergartens. The creation of a series of nature-based curriculum planning books has brought together her two areas of expertise.

Claire's unique approach to planning with and for children, called Floorbooks®, increases child-led inquiries that are centered around the fascinations children find when they learn with nature. The three spaces of "inside", "outside", and "beyond" are mindfully linked to develop skills and confidence in a predominantly natural environment.

In addition to Claire's international and consultancy work, she runs a community interest company, Living Classrooms, through which the virtual nature school is being delivered. Additionally, she set up the International Association of Nature Pedagogy, a professional organization designed to promote and support all forms of nature-based education for children aged 3 - 8 years throughout the world. This includes forest kindergartens, forest schools, nature preschools, and nature kindergartens.

Claire's philanthropic work has had a significant impact around the world. She is part of a leadership group of consultants who make up the World Nature Collaborative, a working party of the World Forum Foundation. The purpose of the group is to develop a cohesive network and approach to experiential learning in outdoor spaces in a variety of climates. The nature collaborative brings together educators, landscape architects, environmentalists, and health workers to support a multidisciplinary approach to outdoor educational provision.

We encourage you to visit www.mindstretchers.academy to download the complimentary *Fascination Series Handbook* that will guide you on how to teach the course virtually and provide you with a shopping list and additional resources to assist you.

Connect with Claire at www.mindstretchers.academy to stay up to date with all of the books in the *Fascination Series* along with additional resources and training.

"The true value of this little gem of a book is that it respects the power of allowing children to have their own adventures, follow their own imaginations and make their own discoveries." ~ Tim Gill

"An invaluable and inspirational resource, by an internationally recognized expert in her field, that beautifully illustrates the power of nature to amplify every dimension of learning." ~ Richard Louv

Printed in Great Britain
by Amazon

40508039R00084